Back to Basics™

YEAR 5

GRAMMAR AND PUNCTUATION

Victoria Hazell

Illustrated by
Janice Bowles

About this book

This book is designed to review the essential Grammar and Punctuation skills required in Year 5.

Each unit begins with a brief **explanation** of a particular grammar or punctuation concept. This is followed by examples of how this concept is used in text **(We practise)**. Parents or carers are encouraged to read the explanation and the **We practise** section together with their child.

Practical exercises are then provided to give your child the opportunity to practise the concept **(You practise)**. These exercises reinforce the concept and check that your child understands it fully.

The two **tests** at the back of the book can be done once the book has been completed. These are designed to check that your child's punctuation and grammar skills are consolidated.

If further instruction is required, we recommend that this book be provided to your child's teacher for review. Then the parent or carer and the teacher can devise a plan to ensure all the basic concepts are fully understood and consolidated.

Meet 'BOB' – Back Of the Book

At the end of each unit, BOB reminds your child to go to the **Answer** section at the Back of the Book to check the answers.

Victoria Hazell

Game Cards Instructions

Possessives

Cut out the cards and then match the eight possessive phrases to the pairs of common and proper nouns that form the phrases. Imagine there is a "belongs to" card for each set created. Sometimes "belongs to" isn't quite the right phrase; try "for" or "of" to get the right meaning.

Meg's bike — bike belongs to Meg
women's club — club for women

Australian Curriculum Year 5

Text structure & organisation

Understand how possession is signalled through apostrophes and how to use apostrophes of possession for common and proper nouns (ACELA1506)

Expressing & developing ideas

Understand the difference between main and subordinate clauses and how these can be combined to create complex sentences through subordinating conjunctions to develop and expand ideas (ACELA1507)

Understand how noun and adjective groups can be expanded in a variety of ways to provide a fuller description of the person, thing or idea (ACELA1508)

Contents & Checklist

PUNCTUATION 1

Capital letter	ABC	To start a sentence and a proper noun.
Full stop	.	To end a sentence.
Question mark	?	To end a question.
Exclamation mark	!	To end an exclamation.
Comma	,	To show the reader when to pause, and to separate items in a list.

Punctuation makes your writing clear and easy to understand.

All the punctuation marks are highlighted in this story.

Did you know that the first submarine was a rowing boat covered with a waterproof skin? Submarines have changed a lot to become the machine we know today. We now have submarines that are powered by nuclear force. A submarine can be as long as two football fields and carry 150 crew! Submarines can now stay underwater for months. Some submarines don't even need a human on board and they can be operated by remote control so that no lives are endangered. Submarines have come a long way since the waterproof rowing boat.

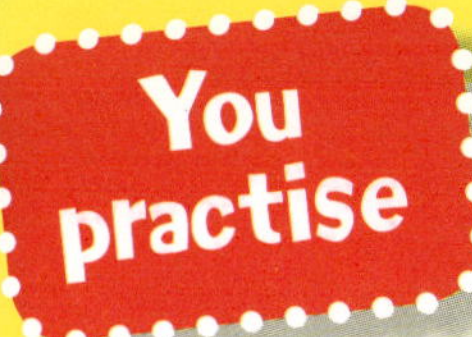

Rewrite this text, adding the correct punctuation.

Fast Flyers

modern fighter planes are high-speed machines why do they need to be because pilots are often flying to places where they are not welcome

____

____

____

____

BOB time!

You practise

Rewrite this text, adding the correct punctuation.

the hornet

the hornet can be a high-flying fighter and it can also attack ground targets the hornet can carry more than 20 kinds of missiles it has a six-barrel cannon in its nose that can shoot 6000 rounds a minute

____

____

____

____

____

BOB Time!

SENTENCE TYPES 1

Sentence A group of words that has meaning.
A sentence starts with a **capital letter** and ends with a **full stop**, **question mark** or **exclamation mark**.
A sentence has to have a **verb** and a **subject**.

The **girl** **ate** the red jelly.

subject verb

Sentences are the building blocks of our language.

There are four types of sentences:

Statement A sentence that tells a fact or an idea, which can be true or false.

Emotion A sentence that expresses emotions or feelings, such as joy or anger.

Command A sentence that makes a command, or an order to do something.

Exclamation A sentence that shows **strong** feelings or emotions and ends with an **exclamation mark**.

We practise

An example of each sentence type is highlighted in a different colour. Red = statement Green = emotion Blue = exclamation Pink = command

I wonder if there are any kids out there that are just like me? Like kids who can't be bothered cleaning their rooms when they are told to? Like kids who have parents that say, "CLEAN YOUR ROOM OR ELSE!"? Like kids who push all their junk under their bed? Well, next time this happens, it's worth thinking about what could happen if you don't clean your room. One time my parents got so mad that they bundled up everything and threw it out the back door! I can't tell you how embarrassing it was when my friends came over and saw all my stuff on the ground. My advice? Clean your room.

You practise

Circle TWO examples of each sentence type in this text. Red = statement Blue = exclamation Green = emotion Pink = command

Mayan Marvels

As they struggled on, the jungle became more treacherous. At times they could barely get a foothold in the soft mud of the rainforest floor. Mia stopped to catch her breath. "This humidity is too much! The jungle is so thick, I don't think we'll ever get there."

After two more agonising hours they finally reached the base of the cliffs. The limestone walls towered above them. Professor Drake slapped Flynn on the back. "Come on, Flynn, this is an easy one. Just watch your footing and hold on tight."

Flynn was determined to conquer this cliff. His spirits soared with each new hold he made. His hands and feet searched for cracks in the rock's surface and he pulled himself higher and higher, until he finally reached the top. Flynn and Mia sat, exhausted. They looked out over the endless jungle edged by a crimson sunset. Professor Drake was already pulling more rope from his backpack. "What's going on?" quizzed Flynn. "There's nothing more to climb!" The professor smiled. "You're right, Flynn, but what goes up must come down. So get ready to go again."

BOB time!

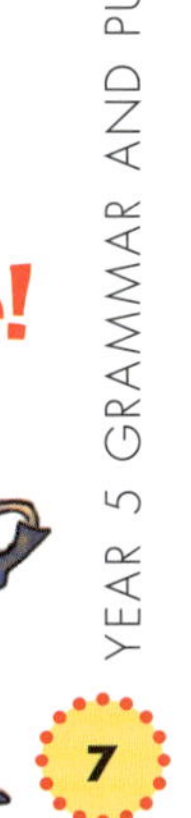

NOUNS AND ADJECTIVES

Common noun A word that names something – a person, an animal, a place, a feeling, a thing or an idea.

Proper noun A word that names a particular person or a special place or thing. A proper noun starts with a capital letter.

Pronoun A word that replaces a noun.

Concrete noun A noun that names people, places and things that you **can** see, touch, hear, taste or smell.

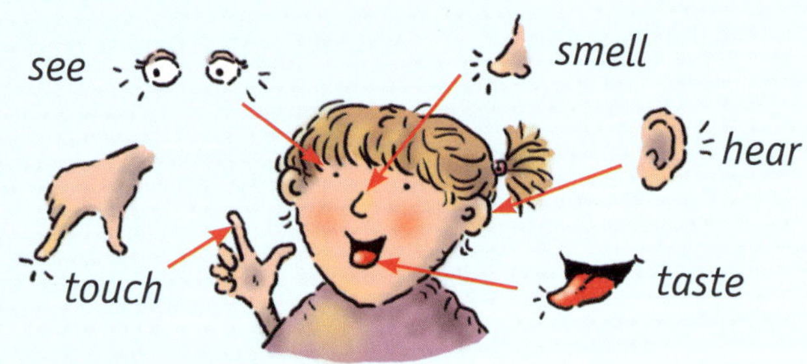

Abstract noun A noun that names emotions and ideas that you **cannot** see, touch, hear, taste or smell.

Adjective A word that describes a noun.

Common nouns name the everyday things around us.

We practise

Let's see if we can find one example of an adjective and each type of noun in this text.

A person who travels in space is called an astronaut. In America there is an agency that trains people to travel into space, it is called NASA. Yuri Gagarin was the first human being to ever travel in space. He did this in 1961. In 1969, the first person to walk on the moon was Neil Armstrong. His first famous words were, "That's one small step for man, one giant leap for mankind."

Common noun	man	**Proper noun**	America
Pronoun	he	**Concrete noun**	astronaut
Abstract noun	space	**Adjective**	first

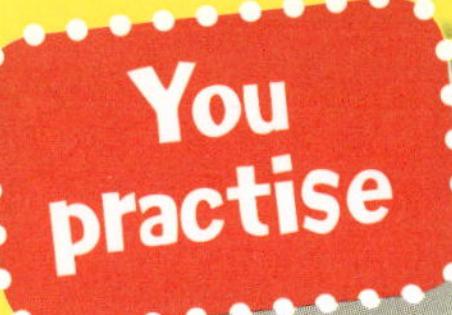

Find TWO examples of an adjective and each type of noun in the text. Write the words below.

Animal Astronauts

Once we knew that rockets could reach space, the race was on to get humans out there. Before scientists dared send a human into space, they needed information about whether a living thing could survive in space. In 1957, the Soviet Union launched the satellite *Sputnik 1* into orbit. When that succeeded, they sent the first living creature into space – a dog named Laika. But there was no way to return the satellite to Earth and Laika died in space.

On 13 December 1958, a squirrel monkey named Gordo was launched into space. The spacecraft was *Jupiter AM-13*. Gordo made a suborbital flight; this means that he reached space, but he did not orbit the Earth. Scientists concluded that Gordo did not suffer any adverse effects. Sadly, however, he died at sea when the spacecraft returned to Earth and splashed down in the ocean.

1 **Adjectives** ______________ ______________

2 **Common nouns** ______________ ______________

3 **Proper nouns** ______________ ______________

4 **Pronouns** ______________ ______________

5 **Concrete nouns** ______________ ______________

6 **Abstract nouns** ______________ ______________

BOB time!

SYNONYMS AND ANTONYMS

Synonym

A word that has a **similar** meaning to another word.

mad – angry

walking – strolling

Antonym

A word that has the **opposite** meaning to another word.

high – low

over – under

We practise

Here are some pairs of antonyms and synonyms.

Antonyms

agree	disagree
sink	float
windy	calm
quiet	noisy
open	closed

Synonyms

boiling	hot
argue	fight
huge	big
father	dad
napping	sleeping

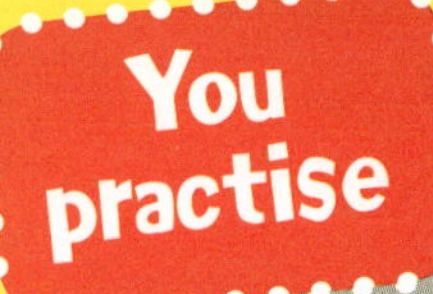

Choose an antonym from the box for each word below.

incorrect loud late enormous hate

quiet	
small	
love	
early	
correct	

BOB time!

You practise

Choose a synonym from the box for each word below.

giggle wealthy push sob seat

rich	
cry	
chair	
laugh	
shove	

BOB time!

UNIT 5 PREFIXES AND SUFFIXES

Prefix

A group of letters added to the **front** of a word to make a new word.

Often the prefix makes a word with the opposite meaning.

im + possible
= **im**possible

un + acceptable
= **un**acceptable

Suffix

A group of letters added to the **end** of a word to make a new word.

strong + *est* = strong**est**
attract + *ive* = attract**ive**

Adding a suffix to a word can also make it into a different part of speech.

loyal + *ty* = loyalty
an **adjective** becomes a **noun**

entertain + *ment* = entertainment
a **verb** becomes a **noun**

Prefix = before
Suffix = after

We practise

A prefix has been added to each word to make a new word.

misinform **dis**advantage **anti**clockwise
realign **de**activate

A suffix has been added to each word to make a new word.

sleep**less** jump**ing** suit**able** walk**ed**
smooth**est**

You practise

Use the prefixes in the box to make new words.

dis	in	im	il	mis

__________mature __________sufficient __________please

__________possible __________logical __________mortal

__________literate __________understood __________appear

__________appoint

BOB time!

You practise

Use the suffixes in the box to make new words.

en	ful	less	ish	ly

fool__________ sharp__________ brave__________

use__________ hope__________ sheep__________

force__________ speech__________ calm__________

forget__________

UNIT 6

CONTRACTIONS

Contraction

A word that has been shortened, or made smaller. Contractions often make two words into one word.

Why? Contracting a word makes it possible to say and write words more easily and quickly.

We usually say **can't** instead of **cannot** because **can't** is easier and quicker to say and write than **cannot**.

Apostrophe of contraction

A punctuation mark (') that shows where letters have been left out of a contraction.

she'll = she will the letters **wi** have been left out

Contractions save time!

Here are some contractions.

you + had = **you'd**

was + not = **wasn't**

we + had = **we'd**

had + not = **hadn't**

could + not = **couldn't**

You practise

What is the correct contraction for each pair of words?

 I + am = ______________________

 you + are = ______________________

 he + is = ______________________

 it + is = ______________________

 we + are = ______________________

BOB time!

You practise

What words have been contracted?

 ______________ + ______________ = you'll

 ______________ + ______________ = they're

 ______________ + ______________ = shouldn't

 ______________ + ______________ = weren't

 ______________ + ______________ = mustn't

BOB time!

SUBJECT AND VERB AGREEMENT

Clause

A group of words that has a **subject** and a **verb**. One clause can be a complete sentence.

The **dog chews** the ball.

subject verb

When you write a clause it is important that the **subject** and the **verb** agree. If the subject is **singular** (one), then the verb must be singular as well.

singular **verb**

The **dog chews** the ball.

singular **subject**

If the subject is **plural** (more than one), then the verb must be plural as well.

plural **verb**

The **dogs chew** the ball.

plural **subject**

Confused? Read the sentence out loud and you will know what sounds right or wrong.

We practise

The correct verb is circled so that the subject and verb agree.

"**Are**/**Is** your brothers coming with us to the beach?"

I **am**/**are** going on holiday next week.

Matt **play**/**plays** soccer with me.

Sophie and Laura **wants**/**want** to go down the slide together.

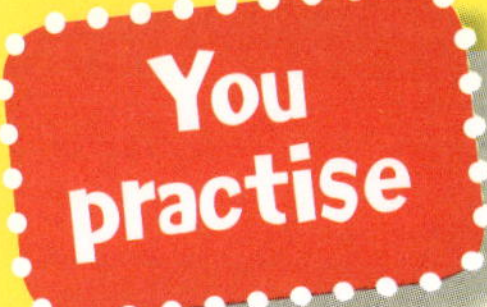

Circle the correct verb so that the subject and verb agree.

The girls **decides/decide** to go home.

The dishes in the sink **is/are** dirty and **need/needs** to be washed.

Bart Simpson **write/writes** lines on the board when he **are/is** naughty.

All the girls in my class at school **play/plays** in the local netball team.

Fish and chips **tastes/taste** even better at the beach!

Circle the correct verb so that the subject and verb agree.

We **am/are** on the bus on our way home from school.

The Doves **are/is** the champions of the netball competition!

We always **celebrate/celebrates** Christmas at Grandma's house.

The grapes in my lunch box **tastes/taste** juicy and sweet.

We **was/were** told to wear our school uniform correctly.

BOB time!

PARAGRAPHS

Paragraph

A group of sentences that are about the same topic. When writing a narrative text, paragraphs help to build the story. A new paragraph can show a change in time, a new setting or introduce another character.

A paragraph starts with a **topic sentence**. This sentence introduces the topic or idea that will be explored in the paragraph.

Don't forget your topic sentence.

These sentences have been put together to make a complete paragraph below. Notice how the topic sentence comes first and then the other sentences follow in a logical order.

Earwigs

They got their name because it was once thought that they could climb into your ear and lay eggs or tunnel into your brain.

Topic sentence: Earwigs are small insects.

This is not true.

They hide during the day.

Earwigs eat leaves, flowers, fruit, mould and even other insects.

Earwigs can be found under piles of lawn clippings or compost, or even in holes in trees.

We practise

Earwigs

Earwigs are small insects. They got their name because it was once thought that they could climb into your ear and lay eggs or tunnel into your brain. This is not true. Earwigs eat leaves, flowers, fruit, mould and even other insects. They hide during the day. Earwigs can be found under piles of lawn clippings or compost, or even in holes in trees.

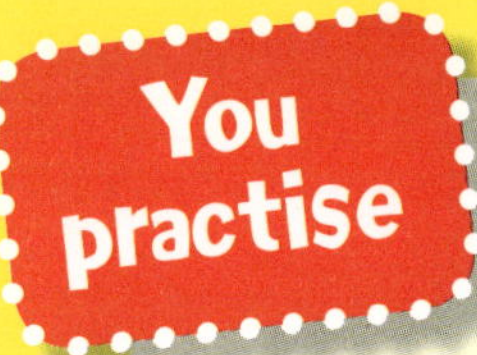

Rewrite these sentences to make a complete paragraph. Make sure the topic sentence comes first and the other sentences follow in a logical order.

Mosquitoes

They also have visual sensors, which means that they are attracted to certain colours.
First, mosquitoes have chemical sensors, which means that they are attracted to certain chemicals.
They do this with three special types of sensors.
Topic sentence: Mosquitoes are insects that have been around for more than 30 million years.
And last, mosquitoes have heat sensors, which means they can find warm-blooded mammals and birds to feed on.
Mosquitoes are very clever at finding their prey.

BOB time!

QUOTATION MARKS

Quotation marks

Punctuation marks that show direct speech (the actual words spoken by someone). Quotation marks are also known as speech marks and they look like this " ".

The **speaker** is shown before or after the quotation marks. A **comma** is often used before the direct speech begins or ends. The direct speech starts with a **capital letter**.

The **punctuation** in the direct speech always goes **inside** the quotation marks.

Quotation marks always come in pairs – " opens the quotation and " closes it.

speaker — quotation marks — direct speech — quotation marks

Mr Hope said, "Wear a hat and put on sunscreen at recess."

comma — capital letter — full stop

The correct punctuation for direct speech is highlighted in each sentence.

"Would you like to come to my house for a sleepover?" asked Franco.

"I am dreading my English exam," said Phil.

Jane said, "I am looking forward to the English exam."

The lady on the train enquired, "Is that seat taken?"

"We won the grand final!" I exclaimed proudly.

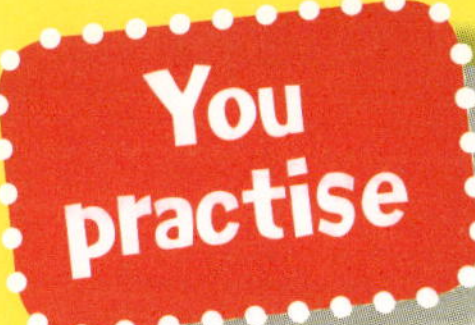

Add the correct punctuation for direct speech in each sentence.

1 My father always said be careful what you wish for

2 i don't care what you think about it the young boy yelled.

3 oh, what a beautiful morning Carly exclaimed.

4 turn left, then right and we are the second house on the left Sophia directed.

5 The teacher asked does anyone have a funny story

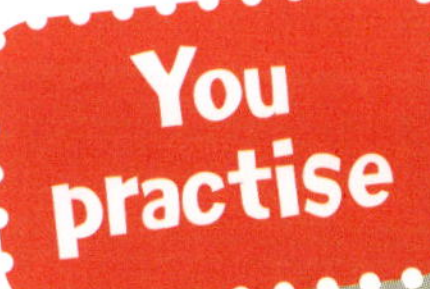

Add the correct punctuation for direct speech in each sentence.

6 do you like green eggs and ham the Cat in the Hat asked the children.

7 The canteen lady announced sorry, but there are no more sausage rolls

8 and they all lived happily ever after the teacher whispered.

9 can we go for a swim at the beach tomorrow the twins pleaded.

10 why did the chicken cross the road Simon asked his friend.

BOB time!

ADVERBIALS

Adverbial

An **adverb**, **phrase** or **clause** that gives more information about a verb.

He **wore** his gum boots **because the ground was muddy.**

↑ verb ↑ adverbial

We have been **climbing** the mountain **for over two hours**.

↑ verb ↑ adverbial

Like an adverb, adverbial phrases and clauses can tell us how, when, where, why or for how long an action happens.

The verb is circled and the adverbial is underlined in the following sentences.

We (washed) our hands after playing outside.

adverbial shows **when** we washed our hands

The piano (fell) down the stairs as we tried to shift it.

adverbial shows **where** the piano fell

You need to (finish) your homework before you watch TV.

adverbial shows **when** you need to finish your homework

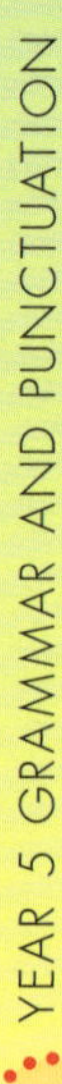

You practise

Underline the adverbial in each sentence. Remember, it gives more information about the verb.

She finally found the cat.

Yesterday I practised for my music lesson.

The scouts toasted marshmallows over the campfire.

Johan pushed his bed over to the window.

Zara buys lunch from the canteen once a week.

BOB time!

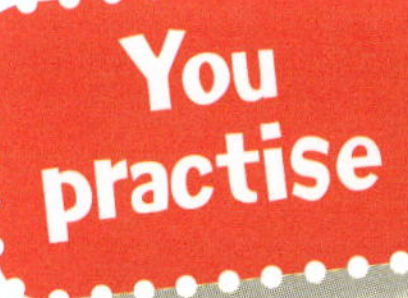

You practise

Underline the adverbial in each sentence. Remember, it gives more information about the verb.

Sam loves swimming on summer afternoons.

I wear a scarf and beanie in the snow.

The creature stared at me with an angry expression.

I'll meet you on the oval at lunchtime.

We hardly ever use the microwave.

BOB time!

APOSTROPHE OF POSSESSION

Apostrophe of possession

A punctuation mark that is used with nouns (and proper nouns) to show ownership or possession.

The **apostrophe of possession** is used with the letter **s**, and it comes **after** the noun and **before** the **s**.

The boy's desk	the desk **belongs** to the boy
Batman's batmobile	the batmobile **belongs** to Batman

However, if the noun is **plural** or **ends in s**, then the apostrophe is placed **after** the **s**.

The dogs' bones James' scooter
The three girls' muddy clothes

Watch out for apostrophes that are used incorrectly:

Banana's for sale X
Yummy hamburger's X

We practise

A possessive apostrophe and the letter 's' are added to the noun to show ownership in each sentence.

Sergio's friends came over to hang out for the afternoon.	the friends **belong** to Sergio
The girl's skateboard was outside the back door.	the skateboard **belongs** to the girl
I put the babies' nappies in their bags.	the nappies **belong** to the babies (plural)
We live above a ladies' hairdressing salon.	the hairdressing salon **belongs** to the ladies (plural)

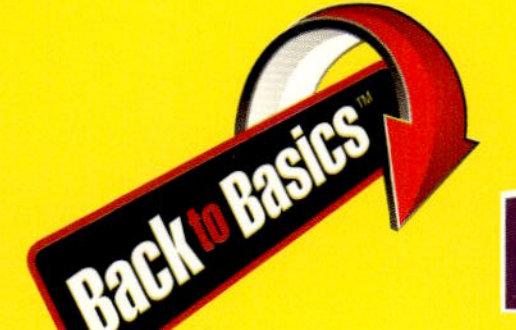

POSSESSIVES

YEAR 5

POSSESSIVES

YEAR 5

POSSESSIVES

YEAR 5

POSSESSIVES

YEAR 5

POSSESSIVES

YEAR 5

POSSESSIVES

YEAR 5

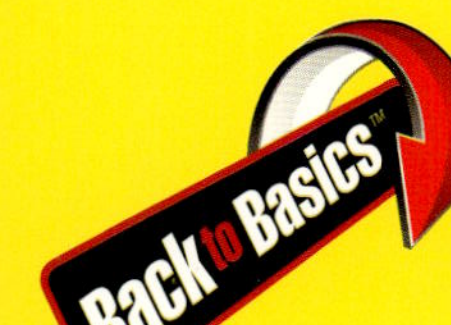

POSSESSIVES

YEAR 5

POSSESSIVES

YEAR 5

POSSESSIVES

YEAR 5

POSSESSIVES

YEAR 5

POSSESSIVES

YEAR 5

POSSESSIVES

YEAR 5

children	teacher	Sonia's birthday
girl	children's movie	boys
boys' game	Tim	bone
Sonia	surfboard	Year 5's teacher

dog	parents' car	skateboard
game	birthday	dog's bone
parents	Tim's skateboard	Year 5
girl's surfboard	car	movie

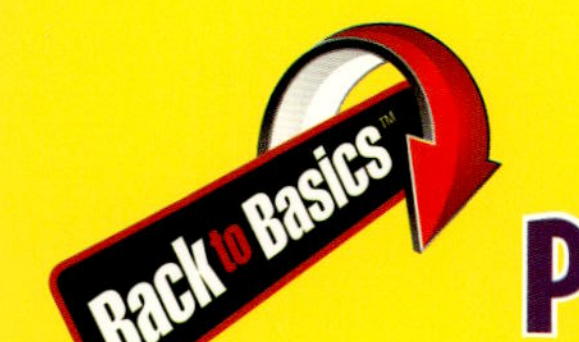

POSSESSIVES

YEAR 5

POSSESSIVES

YEAR 5

POSSESSIVES

YEAR 5

POSSESSIVES

YEAR 5

POSSESSIVES

YEAR 5

POSSESSIVES

YEAR 5

POSSESSIVES

YEAR 5

POSSESSIVES

YEAR 5

POSSESSIVES

YEAR 5

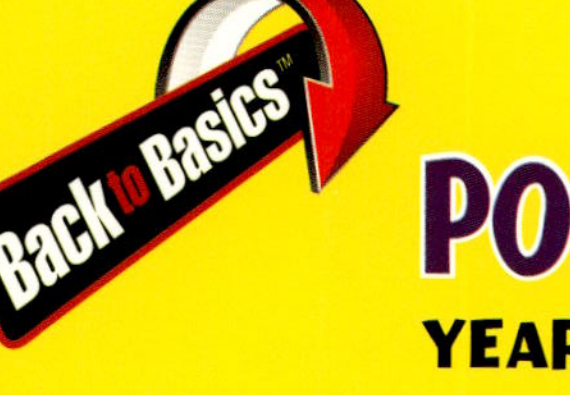

POSSESSIVES

YEAR 5

POSSESSIVES

YEAR 5

POSSESSIVES

YEAR 5

You practise

Add the possessive apostrophe to the noun in each sentence.

1 I took **Peters** plate because he had finished his meal.

2 Put the **dogs** dinner outside for them to eat.

3 I was wondering, is that **James** iPod or yours?

4 The **toddlers** faces are dirty after eating ice-cream.

5 The **mans** beard is very long and dirty.

BOB time!

Add the possessive apostrophe and 's' to the noun in each sentence.

6 My friend___ new car is red and it has seven seats.

7 Both of my brother___ names are hard to pronounce.

8 "Hannah___ new haircut looks great!" Fiona exclaimed.

9 Brendan___ cat is missing.

10 The twin boy___ clothes were covered in mud.

BOB time!

CLAUSES

Subordinating conjunctions include: **after, although, as, because, before, if, since, than, that, though, till, until, when, where** and **while.**

Clause A group of words that are part of a sentence.

There are two types of clauses:

Main clause The essential part of a sentence. It is one complete idea. One main clause can be a simple sentence.

Subordinate clause Gives more information about the idea in the main clause. It is not a complete sentence on its own.

The main and subordinate clauses are linked by a **subordinating conjunction.**

Henry went to the park **because** he loved the slide.

main clause — subordinating conjunction — subordinate clause

Subordinate clauses can make your writing more interesting and descriptive.

The main clause is circled, the subordinate clause is underlined and the subordinating conjunction is highlighted in each sentence.

(I will let you go to the party) **if** you clean your room.

(Moira practised the song) **until** she had learnt it off by heart.

(He left the house) **because** he was going to the movies.

(He felt much better) **after** he had finished the test.

We practise

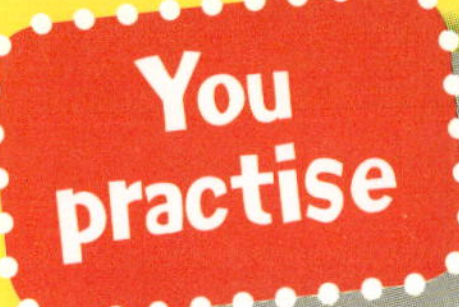

Circle the main clause and underline the subordinate clause in each sentence.

1. The truck slowed down before it reached the red light.
2. Sharon screamed at the top of her voice when she saw the dark shadow.
3. Mrs Lee scolded her children because they behaved badly.
4. We are going to the beach tomorrow unless it is raining.
5. Jenny ate the popcorn while she watched the movie.

BOB time!

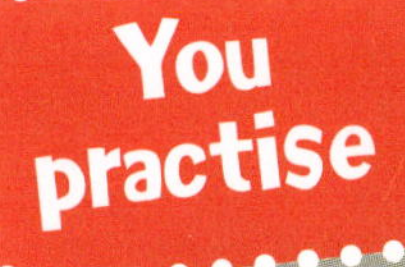

Write a subordinate clause after each subordinating conjunction.

6. You cannot have dessert unless ____________________.

7. We had dinner before ____________________.

8. We went for a walk even though ____________________.

9. The dog barked whenever ____________________.

10. I will ice the cupcakes when ____________________.

UNIT 13

NOUN GROUPS

A noun group adds more information about the **noun** in a sentence.

Noun group

A noun with extra words that describe or add meaning to the noun. These words are called **descriptors**.

the lush green **grass** = descriptors + noun
the lush green describe the noun **grass**

my good **friend**	descriptors + noun
a few naughty **kids**	descriptors + noun
the long wooden **table**	descriptors + noun
the incredibly loud **music**	descriptors + noun
that crowd of **people**	descriptors + noun
children from our **class**	noun + descriptors

We practise

One noun group is underlined in each sentence.

The fishermen caught about fifteen big fish that afternoon.

The flock of seagulls swooped down on the bread crusts.

A couple of sneaky thieves hid in the bushes.

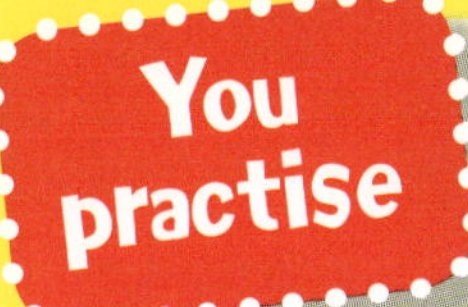

Underline one noun group in each sentence.

 Some vicious-sounding **dogs** were barking outside last night.

 The uniformed police **inspector** asked many questions.

 The yellow and green **flag** was flapping in the breeze.

 A few of the local **kids** helped to clean up the mess.

 The old blue denim **jeans** were her favourite pair.

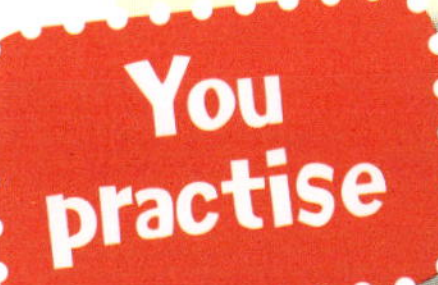

Underline one noun group in each sentence.

 A small group of **children** wandered around the museum.

 Four **netballs** were needed for training.

 A long line of **ants** crawled along the kitchen bench.

 Many **people** like to relax and watch TV.

 My whole **class** is entering the science competition.

ADJECTIVE GROUPS

Adjective group

An **adjective** or adjectives that give more information about the noun (or pronoun).

The **dog**

You can add **adjectives** to give more information about the **noun** dog.

The black **dog**	adjective + noun
The big, black, spotty **dog**	adjectives + noun

The words **big, black, spotty** give more information about the dog.

We practise

The adjective group is underlined in each sentence.

Iceblocks are <u>so cool and refreshing</u>.

cool and **refreshing** add more information about **iceblocks**

She wore a <u>long, pink, frilly</u> **dress**.

long, **pink** and **frilly** add more information about the **dress**

She is a <u>very smart and interesting</u> **person**.

very smart and **interesting** add more about **her**

You practise **Underline one adjective group in each sentence.**

 1 The **teacher** is a kind, caring woman.

 2 We crossed the enormously high **bridge**.

 3 The brave **warrior** belonged to another tribe.

 4 These are the most beautiful **roses** I have ever seen.

 5 He walked through the muddy **street**.

BOB time!

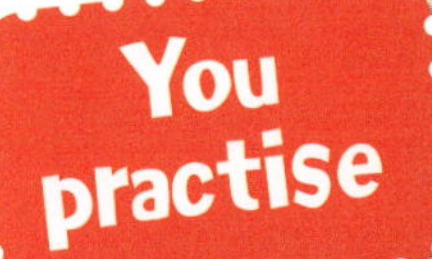

Underline one adjective group in each sentence.

 6 The injured **player** was in intense pain.

 7 The **twins** were like two peas in a pod.

 8 The umpire said that the **play** was unduly rough.

 9 That year **Australia** had more than expected rainfall.

 10 It was incredibly **important** that he contact his grandmother.

BOB time!

COLONS AND SEMICOLONS

Colon :

A punctuation mark used to **introduce** a list of items or extra information.

In her beach bag she carried: a towel, sunscreen, a hat, a shirt and a drink.

Semicolon ;

A punctuation mark used to **separate** two **main clauses**.

Frank rides his scooter; his sister rides a skateboard.

We practise

A colon or semicolon is added to these sentences.

In the picnic hamper we packed: ham rolls, fruit, drinks and some cake.

Collect the following ingredients: milk, flour, eggs and sugar.

It was a windy Saturday afternoon; our kite tossed and turned in the sky.

The lake was covered in mist; it looked spooky and mysterious.

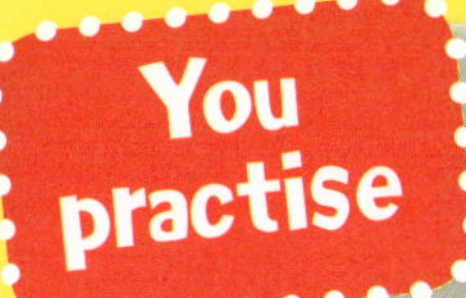

Add a colon or a semicolon to each sentence.

1. In her bag she had scissors, a hairbrush and her address book.

2. Dad hates going to bed early there is so much to watch on the telly.

3. We are moving to New Zealand we love the outdoor life.

4. My favourite cereals are Corn Flakes, Frosties and Weet-Bix.

5. We are not going on holiday this year flights are so expensive.

BOB time!

Add a colon or a semicolon to each sentence.

6. For breakfast I would like sausages, beans, eggs and bacon.

7. Tim recently took up the guitar he is a natural musician.

8. The three largest earthquakes occurred in San Francisco, Tokyo and Lima.

9. The canteen is closed please return to the classroom.

10. To be healthy we need three things rest, a good diet and exercise.

BOB time!

HYPHENS AND DASHES

Hyphen A punctuation mark used to join compound words, to attach prefixes and to avoid confusion.

one-way easy-going well-dressed old-fashioned

ex-wife pre-owned cross-reference

re-enter (not reenter) re-creation (not recreation)

Dash A punctuation mark used to show a sudden change of thought in a sentence. A dash can also separate non-essential elements in a sentence. A dash is longer than a hyphen.

Let's get together for dinner – or perhaps you would prefer we talk on the phone.

She looked at the sea – the golden sand, wild waves, crystal clear water – and smiled.

Who would have thought the dash was longer than the hyphen?

Look at how the hyphen or the dash is used in each sentence.

We practise

The five-year-old girl is about to start school.
hyphen in a compound word

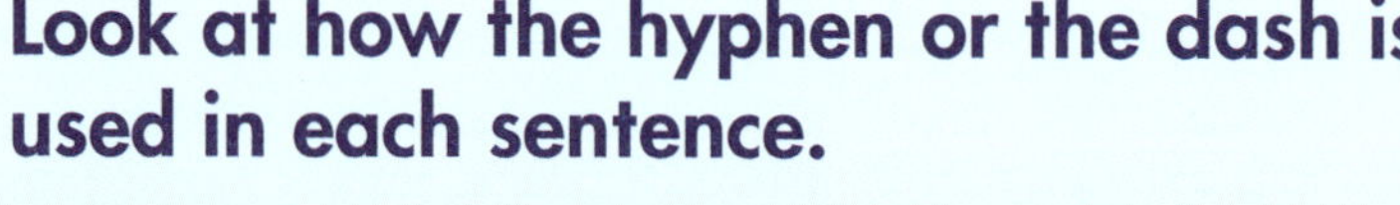

The girls want to play netball – or so they say.
dash to show a sudden change of thought

It was a bad movie – too long, boring and violent – and I don't recommend it.
dash to separate non-essential information

It was three-thirty in the afternoon when the school bell rang.
hyphen in a compound word

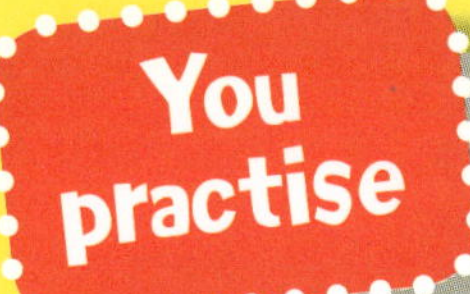

Add a hyphen or a dash to each sentence.

I am still friends with my ex girlfriend.

I am thinking of re covering my lounge chairs.

He said that he would go and he did.

I have seventy nine footy cards.

My friends Paul, Barry and Homer all love apple crumble.

BOB time!

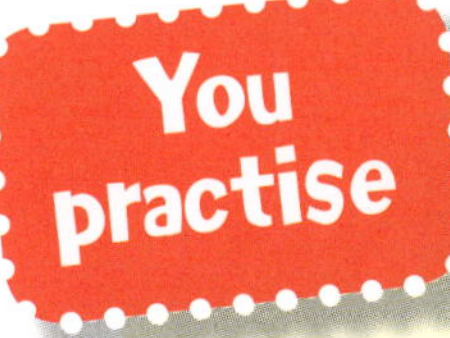

Add a hyphen or a dash to each sentence.

He won the 100 metre race.

I love breakfast bacon, eggs, toast, everything it's my favourite meal.

My co workers sang happy birthday to me.

He thought long and hard this decision could change his life!

We went north east on our bush walk.

BOB time!

HOMOPHONES AND HOMOGRAPHS

Homophone A word that **sounds the same** as another word, but has a **different spelling** and a **different meaning**.

flower  **flour** 

Homograph A word that has the **same spelling** as another word, but has a **different meaning** (and sometimes also with a **different sound**, or pronunciation).

kid  **kid** 

We practise

Are these words homophones or homographs?

I threw the **ball** to the dog.
She wore her long gown to the **ball**.
homographs because they have same spelling but a different meaning

My pants are too tight around my **waist**.
Most packaging is a **waste** of paper and plastic.
homophones because they sound the same but have a different spelling and a different meaning

Just wait, I'll be ready in **minute**!
I made sure every **minute** detail was correct.
homographs because they have same spelling but a different meaning (and a different sound)

You practise

Circle the correct homophone in each sentence.

1. The **principle/principal** spoke at the school assembly.

2. I would love a **piece/peace** of cake.

3. The **sole/soul** of my shoe has a hole.

4. You can buy **cheap/cheep** apples at the market.

5. She poured too much milk on her **cereal/serial**.

BOB time!

You practise

Choose the correct homograph from the box to complete each pair of sentences.

bear	fair	present	tear	wound

6. The sad movie brought a _______________ to her eye.
I had to patch the _______________ in my skirt.

7. I _______________ the watch because it was slow.
I had a _______________ on my knee from the accident.

8. I thought the umpire's decision was very _______________.
We have a school _______________ every year.

9. I gave my sister her birthday _______________.
Everyone was _______________ at the wedding.

BOB time!

10. The large _______________ growled loudly.
I don't think I can _______________ it any longer.

PARTS OF SPEECH

Common noun Names a person, an animal, a place, a feeling, a thing or even an idea.

Proper noun Names a particular person or a special place or thing. It starts with a capital letter.

Concrete noun Names people, places and things that you can see, touch, hear, taste or smell.

Abstract noun Names emotions, feelings or ideas that you cannot see, touch, hear, taste or smell.

Pronoun Replaces a noun.

Adjective Describes a noun

Verb Shows action.

Adverb Adds meaning to a verb or describes 'how' an action is done.

Conjunction Joining word – joins the two parts of a sentence.

We practise

Let's find one of each of the parts of speech in this text.

The alarm clock blared. Six-thirty am. It was time. Time to get out of my warm bed and begin the training that would one day hopefully make me an Olympic champion. I pulled on my bathers, my tracksuit, runners and grabbed my bike helmet. After a ten-minute ride, I was into the pool, swimming steadily the first of a hundred laps. Some day I will represent Australia at the Olympics. Some day my dream will come true.

Common noun	Proper noun	Concrete noun	Abstract noun	Pronoun	Adjective	Verb	Adverb	Conjunction
clock	Australia	pool	dream	I	warm	swimming	steadily	and

You practise

Find one example of each part of speech in the following text. Write your answers below.

Max My Mate

It was a warm, sunny Saturday and I felt very excited. I was going to the lost dogs' home to choose my best friend. This is the place where dumped dogs end up, kind of like death row. Three weeks to live unless someone wants you. If not, well … it's all over red rover.

As I looked at the dogs, one caught my eye. His coat was kind of red and his eyes seemed to say, "Me! Me!". The person at the home told me he was part red heeler – just like the cattle dogs you see rounding up sheep for farmers. This dog seemed desperate for me to take him home. So I did.

I decided to call him Max. It seemed like a cool name for a dog. As we drove slowly home, Max walked up and down the back seat. He put his head out the window. He nuzzled his cold, wet nose into my neck. Maybe it was his way of saying thanks. Thanks for noticing me. Thanks for saving me from death row. We were both lucky, now we had each other.

Common noun	Proper noun	Concrete noun
Abstract noun	**Pronoun**	**Adjective**
Verb	**Adverb**	**Conjunction**

BOB time!

SENTENCE TYPES 2

Sentence

A group of words that has meaning. A sentence has to have a **verb** and a **subject**.

There are four types of sentences:

Statement A sentence that tells a fact or an idea, which can be true or false.

Emotion A sentence that expresses emotions or feelings, such as joy or anger.

Command A sentence that makes a command, or an order to do something.

Exclamation A sentence that shows **strong** feelings or emotions and ends with an **exclamation mark**.

Let's find one example of each sentence type in this text.

"Come on, get out of bed. It's time to get ready for school. If you don't get a move on you will be late!" This was the cry from my parents each and every day before school. I remember it well. And now I can hear that exasperated plea again. "Come on, get out of bed. It's time to get ready for school. If you don't get a move on you will be late!" The only difference is that now it is my husband calling me and now I am the school principal.

Statement It's time to get ready for school.
Exclamation If you don't get a move on you will be late!
Emotion And now I can hear that exasperated plea again.
Command Come on, get out of bed.

We practise

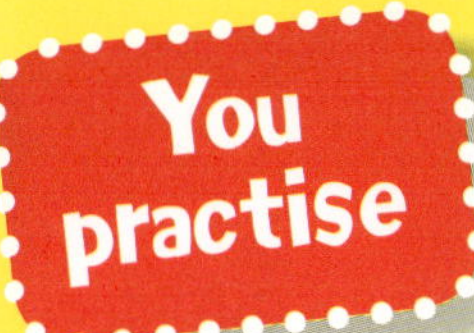

Find one example of each sentence type in this text. Write the sentences below.

BEWARE (The Ballad of Edward or Ned)

Now here is a story that is rarely told
About young Edward who became quite bold
When his mother told him, "No Ned! No!"
He would ignore her and go, yes go!
Because Ned did not want to know

The sign said to, "Swim between the flags"
Mum read it out loud, as she put down their bags
But Edward decided to jump in elsewhere
And tried to swim where the sign said, "Beware"
Because Ned never did take much care

Swept up by a wave, Edward felt himself flip
As he was drawn up into a powerful rip,
It sucked him in and dragged him away
And he nearly drowned, far out in the bay
Because Ned was unlucky that day

It was Mum who noticed that Ned was in trouble
And sent lifeguards to rescue him on the double
Ned was saved, but he was never the same
He grew up fast and improved his game
Because Ned became Edward again

BOB time!

Statement

Exclamation

Emotion

Command

PUNCTUATION 2

Question mark	Ends a question.
Exclamation mark	Ends an exclamation.
Comma	Shows the reader when to pause and separates items in a list.
Apostrophe of contraction	Shows where letters have been left out of a contraction.
Apostrophe of possession	Shows ownership or possession.
Quotation marks	Show direct speech.
Hyphen	Joins compound words, attaches prefixes and avoids confusion.
Dash	Shows a sudden change of thought and separates non-essential elements.
Colon	Introduces a list of items.
Semicolon	Separates two main clauses.

We practise

These punctuation marks are highlighted in this text.

One dark and dreary night there was a knock at the door. We ignored it as our parents had told us never to open the door when they were out. We were not allowed to answer the phone either. The knocking became louder and more frantic – we ignored it. We knew the rules. Then the phone rang, but we didn't pick up. These were our parents' rules. The phone rang again and the knocking continued; we were starting to feel a little afraid. We had two options: continue to ignore or try to find out who was there.

Finally my brother couldn't take it any more. "Who is it?" he yelled. "It's mum and dad! The car has broken-down and we are wet and cold. Now open the door!"

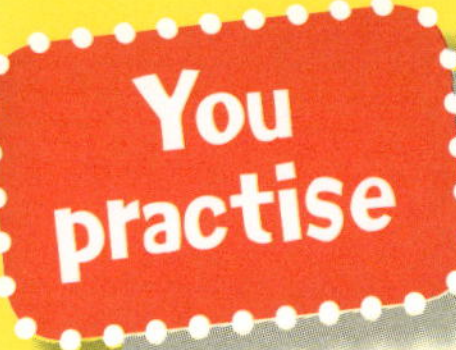

Circle the following punctuation marks in this story.

Question mark Exclamation mark Comma
Apostrophe of contraction Apostrophe of possession
Quotation marks Hyphen Dash Colon Semicolon

Hide Till Day Time

The journey back to the escalator seemed even longer. But it was not so frightening, for she was now fairly sure there was no one on the first floor. This meant the man must be higher – nearer to George. Up Agatha went, on all fours again. The stairs hurt her knees. She didn't stop to see if she was on the second floor, but crawled around to see the next set of escalators and went on up. She reached the third floor just as the man came up with the scooter. He was putting it quietly back, in an out-of-the-way place. She saw the torch's beam: a long wavering streak of bright light. It was coming towards her! Then she heard the footsteps as well. She had just stepped on the floor from the escalator, but now she froze. To go up meant that sooner or later the torch would be sure to shine on her.

She began to back away very slowly from the escalator she had just climbed. But the torch, wavering about as the man steered the scooter, caught her head and shoulders. Her shadow, moving, fell sharply on the floor in front of her; at once the torch became still.

"Who's there?" said the man.

By Joan Phipson

BOB time!

PUNCTUATION TEST

A Funny Thing Happened on the Way to School

"Well Miss, it all happened in the blink of an eye, and let me tell you I was frightened. Frightened for my life. I knew not to worry about my homework, that you would understand and would just be relieved that I was okay," blurted Samuel in response to the invitation for all students to hand in their homework.

"What exactly happened Sam? I am sure you are ready, willing and able to tell us the story," asked Miss Dryden.

"I am happy to oblige Miss. You see it was like this. I was walking along the footpath about two blocks from school. There were two of them, boys from another school, wearing a different uniform. All of a sudden I felt a tremendous thud in the back. Before I knew what was what, they had grabbed my bag and were running away with it! Goodness only knows why Miss. I knew it couldn't be for my lunch: a cheese sandwich, apple and water. So I figured that it was for the one-in-a-million, amazing story I had written for you last night. It was a real original Miss. All about a boy wizard, his name was Henry. Henry's school is called Hagwoots; it's a special wizard school. He has all these amazing adventures where he must use his magic to save the day. I think it is going to be my best story ever! These boys must have got wind of it – after all, it could be a masterpiece. I am thinking movies, merchandise, that sort of thing. So, they thought it could make them millionaires – that's why they did it, I'm sure."

"Well Sam, you can certainly tell a good story, I will give you that. And just so that your talent does not go to waste, you can stay in at lunchtime and write me a new story. But don't worry, I will make sure no one steals this one from you!"

Circle one of each of these in the text.

Question mark	/1
Exclamation mark	/1
Quotation marks	/1
Comma to show a pause	/1
Apostrophe of contraction	/1
Apostrophe of possession	/1
Colon	/1
Semicolon	/1
Hyphen	/1
Dash	/1
Total	**/10**

GRAMMAR TEST

Write one example of each of the following:

Proper noun ______________________ /½

Common noun ______________________ /½

Pronoun ______________________ /½

Adjective ______________________ /½

Statement ______________________________________ /½

Emotion ______________________________________ /½

Command ______________________________________ /½

Exclamation ______________________________________ /½

Circle the adverbial in this sentence. /1

We put our sunscreen and hats on before going to the beach.

Add a subordinating conjunction and a subordinate clause to this sentence. /1

It was a hot summer's day ______________________________

____

Circle the subject and underline the verb in this clause. /1

The clown rides his tricycle around the stage.

Underline one noun group in this sentence. /1

The cold, driving rain lashed steadily at the window.

Circle the correct homophone in this sentence. /1

There/They're all going to the park together.

What homograph could be used in both of these sentences? /1

The gusty ______________ blew all our washing off the line.

I had to ______________ the grandfather clock once a week.

Total /10

ANSWERS

Unit 1

Modern fighter planes are high-speed machines**. W**hy do they need to be**? B**ecause pilots are often flying to places where they are not welcome**.**

The **H**ornet

The hornet can be a high-flying fighter and it can also attack ground targets**. T**he hornet can carry more than 20 kinds of missiles**. I**t has a six-barrel cannon in its nose that can shoot 6000 rounds a minute**!**

Unit 2

Answers will vary.

Statement: Mia stopped to catch her breath. The limestone walls towered above them.

Exclamation: This humidity is too much! There's nothing more to climb!

Emotion: After two more agonising hours they finally reached the base of the cliffs. His spirits soared with each new hold he made.

Command: Just watch your footing and hold on tight. So get ready to go again.

Unit 3

Answers will vary.

Adjectives living, suborbital, adverse

Common nouns rockets, race, humans, scientists, living thing, satellite, orbit, dog, monkey, spacecraft, sea, ocean, race

Proper nouns Soviet Union, *Sputnik 1*, Laika, Earth, Gordo, *Jupiter AM-13*

Pronouns we, they, he

Concrete nouns rockets, race, humans, scientists, living thing, satellite, dog, monkey, spacecraft, sea, ocean

Abstract nouns space, orbit, effects, information

Unit 4

quiet	loud	rich	wealthy
small	enormous	cry	sob
love	hate	chair	seat
early	late	laugh	giggle
correct	incorrect	shove	push

Unit 5

immature	**in**sufficient	**dis**please
impossible	**il**logical	**im**mortal
illiterate	**mis**understood	**dis**appear
disappoint	fool**ish**	sharp**en**
brave**ly**	use**ful**/use**less**	hope**less**/hope**ful**
sheep**ish**	force**ful**	speech**less**
calm**ly**	forget**ful**	

Unit 6

1 I'm
2 you're
3 he's
4 it's
5 we're
6 you will
7 they are
8 should not
9 were not
10 must not

Unit 7

1 decide
2 are, need
3 writes, is
4 play
5 taste
6 are
7 are
8 celebrate
9 taste
10 were

Unit 8

Mosquitoes are insects that have been around for more than 30 million years. Mosquitoes are very clever at finding their prey. They do this with three special types of sensors. First, mosquitoes have chemical sensors, which means that they are attracted to certain chemicals. They also have visual sensors, which means that they are attracted to certain colours. And last, mosquitoes have heat sensors, which means they can find warm-blooded mammals and birds to feed on.

Unit 9

1 My father always said**, "B**e careful what you wish for**."**
2 **"I** don't care what you think about it**!"** the young boy yelled.
3 **"O**h, what a beautiful morning**,"** Carly exclaimed.
4 **"T**urn left, then right and we are the second house on the left**,"** Sophia directed.
5 The teacher asked, **"D**oes anyone have a funny story**?"**
6 **"D**o you like green eggs and ham**?"** the Cat in the Hat asked the children.
7 The canteen lady announced**, "S**orry, but there are no more sausage rolls**."**
8 **"A**nd they all lived happily ever after**,"** the teacher whispered.
9 **"C**an we go for a swim at the beach tomorrow**?"** the twins pleaded.
10 **"W**hy did the chicken cross the road**?"** Simon asked his friend.

ANSWERS

Unit 10

1 She finally found the cat.
2 Yesterday I practised for my music lesson.
3 The scouts toasted marshmallows over the campfire.
4 Johan pushed his bed over to the window.
5 Zara buys lunch from the canteen once a week.
6 Sam loves swimming on summer afternoons.
7 I wear a scarf and beanie in the snow.
8 The creature stared at me with an angry expression.
9 I'll meet you on the oval at lunchtime.
10 We hardly ever use the microwave.

Unit 11

1 Peter's
2 dogs'
3 James'
4 toddlers'
5 man's
6 friend's
7 brothers'
8 Hannah's
9 Brendan's
10 boys'

Unit 12

1 **main: The truck slowed down**
conjunction: before
subordinate: it reached the red light.
2 **main: Sharon screamed at the top of her voice**
conjunction: when
subordinate: she saw the dark shadow.
3 **main: Mrs Lee scolded her children**
conjunction: because
subordinate: they behaved badly.
4 **main: We are going to the beach tomorrow**
conjunction: unless
subordinate: it is raining.
5 **main: Jenny ate the popcorn**
conjunction: while
subordinate: she watched the movie.
6-10 Answers will vary.

Unit 13

1 Some vicious-sounding **dogs** were barking outside last night.
2 The uniformed police **inspector** asked many questions.
3 The yellow and green **flag** was flapping in the breeze
4 A few of the local **kids** helped to clean up the mess.
5 The old blue denim **jeans** were her favourite pair.
6 A small group of **children** wandered around the museum.
7 Four **netballs** were needed for training.
8 A long line of **ants** crawled along the kitchen bench.
9 Many **people** like to relax and watch TV.
10 My whole **class** is entering the science competition.

Unit 14

1 The **teacher** is a kind, caring woman.
2 We crossed the enormously high **bridge**.
3 The brave **warrior** belonged to another tribe.
4 These are the most beautiful **roses** I have ever seen.
5 He walked through the muddy **street**.
6 The injured **player** was in intense pain.
7 The **twins** were like two peas in a pod.
8 The umpire said that the **play** was unduly rough.
9 That year **Australia** had more than expected rainfall.
10 It was incredibly **important** that he contact his grandmother.

Unit 15

1 In her bag she had: scissors, a hairbrush and her address book.
2 Dad hates going to bed early; there is so much to watch on the telly.
3 We are moving to New Zealand; we love the outdoor life.
4 My favourite cereals are: Corn Flakes, Frosties and Weet-Bix.
5 We are not going on holiday this year; flights are so expensive.
6 For breakfast I would like: sausages, beans, eggs and bacon.
7 Tim recently took up the guitar; he is a natural musician.
8 The three largest earthquakes occurred in: San Francisco, Tokyo and Lima.
9 The canteen is closed; please return to the classroom.
10 To be healthy we need three things: rest, a good diet and exercise.

Unit 16

1 I am still friends with my ex-girlfriend.
2 I am thinking of re-covering my lounge chairs.
3 He said that he would go – and he did.
4 I have seventy-nine footy cards.
5 My friends – Paul, Barry and Homer – all love apple crumble.
6 He won the 100-metre race.
7 I love breakfast – bacon, eggs, toast, everything – it's my favourite meal.
8 My co-workers sang happy birthday to me.

ANSWERS

9 He thought long and hard – this decision could change his life!
10 We went north-east on our bush walk.

Unit 17

1 principal
2 piece
3 sole
4 cheap
5 cereal
6 tear
7 wound
8 fair
9 present
10 bear

Unit 18

Answers will vary.
Common noun: friend, place, dog, weeks, coat, eyes, person, sheep, farmers, home, name, seat, head, window, nose, neck
Proper noun: Saturday, Max
Concrete noun: morning, friend, place, dog, coat, eyes, person, sheep, farmers, seat, head, window, nose, neck
Abstract noun: Saturday, death row, weeks
Pronoun: it, I, you, me, he, him, we
Adjective: warm, sunny, lost, best, dumped, three, red, cool, cold, wet, lucky
Verb: felt, excited, choose, live, wants, over, looked, caught, call, told, see, rounding up, seemed, desperate, take, decided, drove, walked, put, nuzzled, saying, noticing, saving
Adverb: very, slowly, both
Conjunction: and, unless

Unit 19

Answers will vary.
Statement: But Edward decided to jump in elsewhere
Exclamation: No Ned! No!
Emotion: Because Ned was unlucky that day
Command: Swim between the flags

Unit 20

Question mark Who's there?
Exclamation mark It was coming towards her!
Comma Up Agatha went, on all fours again
Apostrophe of contraction didn't
Apostrophe of possession torch's
Quotation marks "Who's there?"
Hyphen out-of-the-way
Dash … higher – nearer …
Colon … beam: a long …
Semicolon … front of her; at once the …

Punctuation Test

Answers will vary.
Question mark What exactly happened Sam?
Exclamation mark I think it is going to be my best story ever!
Quotation marks "Well Miss …
Comma to show a pause … of an eye, and let me tell you …
Apostrophe of contraction couldn't
Apostrophe of possession Henry's
Colon … lunch: a cheese …
Semicolon … Hagwoots; it's …
Hyphen one-in-a-million
Dash … wind of it – after all …

Grammar Test

adverbial: before going to the beach.
subject: clown **verb:** rides
noun group: The cold, driving rain
homophone: They're
homograph: wind

Game card answers

girl's surfboard: surfboard *belongs to* girl
parents' car: car *belongs to* parents
Tim's skateboard: skateboard *belongs to* Tim
dog's bone: bone *belongs to* dog
boys' game: game *being played by* boys
children's movie: movie *for* children
Sonia's birthday: birthday *of* Sonia
Year 5's teacher: teacher *of* Year 5